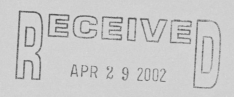

Taekwondo

'Highly recommended reading for any aspiring martial artist. This series will enhance your knowledge of styles, history, grading systems and finding and analyzing the right club.'

Stan 'The Man' Longinidis
8-times World Kickboxing Champion

PAUL COLLINS

This edition first published in 2002 in the United States of America by Chelsea House Publishers, a subsidiary of Haights Cross Communications.

Chelsea House Publishers
1974 Sproul Road, Suite 400
Broomall, PA 19008-0914

The Chelsea House world wide web address is www.chelseahouse.com

Library of Congress Cataloging-in-Publication Data Applied for.

ISBN 0-7910-6554-5

First published in 2000 by
Macmillan Education Australia Pty Ltd
627 Chapel Street, South Yarra, Australia, 3141

Copyright © Paul Collins 2000

Text design and page layout by Judith Summerfeldt-Grace
Cover design by Judith Summerfeldt-Grace

Printed in Hong Kong

Acknowledgements
Photographs by Nick Sandalis, pp. 4, 5, 6, 12, 13, 16, 18, 19, 20, 21, 22, 23, 24, 25; Rod Black, p. 15; Chris Parks, pp. 11, 30 (right); John Smolcic, pp. 7, 30 (left), Geostock p. 9.

The author would like to thank Rod Black, 6th Dan, Chief Instructor Black Taekwondo WTF, and his club for the photos in this book. Rod is a former Australian and State Champion, and a USA championships gold medallist. Rod is the head of the Victorian Coaching Board and the State Tournament Director.

Techniques used in this book should only be practiced under qualified supervision.

Contents

What are martial arts?

The main martial arts

Aikido (Japan)

Hapkido (Korea)

Judo (Japan)

Jujitsu (Japan)

Karate (Japan)

Kendo (Japan)

Kung fu (China)

Muay Thai/Kickboxing
(Thailand)

Ninjutsu (Japan)

Samurai (Japan)

Sumo wrestling (Japan)

Taekwondo (Korea)

Tai Chi (China)

Most people have seen at least one fantastic martial arts movie. A lot of it is trick photography. A **ninja** can not really jump backwards and land on the roof of a towering house! Then again, martial arts is about belief — belief in yourself and your ability to overcome any obstacle, no matter how big or small.

Ask any martial arts student why they train and the answer will be to learn **self-defense**. But that answer only scratches the surface of the term 'martial arts'.

One of the many functions of martial arts is to train students, both physically and mentally.

Martial arts has an ancient tradition that is steeped in discipline and dedication. Most martial arts have developed from ancient Asian combat skills. In **feudal** times, people in Asia had to defend themselves against attack. Quite often, peasants were not allowed to carry weapons, so self-defense became their weapon.

Some martial arts are fighting sports, such as karate and kung fu. Other martial arts concentrate on self-improvement, although self-defense is part of the training. These martial arts, like judo and taekwondo, share the syllable *do*. Do means 'the way to **enlightenment**'.

Kung fu

Judo

Karate

Dedication and discipline

Taekwondo is hard work. Ask any senior student. On average, it takes at least three-and-a-half years to reach black belt status, and even then there is a lot more to learn.

Dedication plays a major role in the life of a martial arts student. Training can be up to four times a week, and an average session lasts from 60 to 90 minutes.

Students practice one simple procedure over and over again. They might repeat a simple move 20 times in one night, only to repeat the same move the next time they train. Martial artists learn through repetition, so that even the most basic moves can be automatically performed when they are suddenly required.

A student practicing simple moves.

Taekwondo

Understanding taekwondo

The Ten Commandments of Taekwondo

1 Loyalty to your country

2 Respect your parents

3 Faithfulness to your spouse

4 Respect your brothers and sisters

5 Loyalty to your friends

6 Respect your elders

7 Respect your teacher

8 **Indomitable** spirit

9 Loyalty to your school

10 Finish what you begin

The spectacular aerial kicks in taekwondo were originally developed for fighters on foot to knock warriors off their horses.

Taekwondo is well-known for its powerful flying kicks.

Korea: the birthplace of taekwondo

Population:	**70 million**
Language:	**Korean**
Currency:	**Won (W)**
Main Religions:	**Taoism and Buddhism**

*The South Korean flag.
The **Yin and Yang**
emblem in the center of
the flag is familiar to most
martial artists. The Yin and
the Yang represent the
feminine and the
masculine energies in
martial arts. The Yin can
be explained as flowing
and fluid, as in performing
patterns and good
technique. The Yang might
be the power and the
force of sparring with a
partner. Martial arts need
both opposing energies,
the Yin and the Yang. The
four black symbols, one in
each corner, represent
Heaven, Earth, Fire and
Water.*

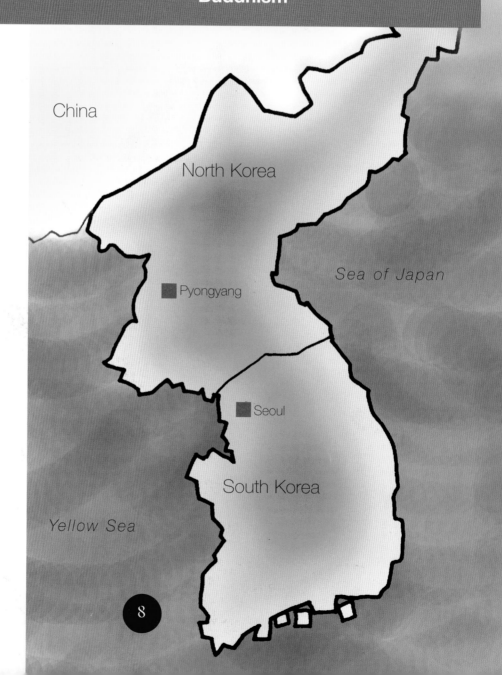

Korea was once a single country in north-eastern Asia. It formed a mountainous peninsula situated between the Yellow Sea and the Sea of Japan.

The Japanese invaded Korea in 1910 and occupied it until 1945, when they were defeated in World War II. After World War II, Korea was occupied in the north by Soviet (Russian) troops and in the south by troops from the United States of America.

In 1948, elections were held but the North would not take part in these elections. Korea then divided into two countries: North Korea (The Democratic People's Republic of Korea) and South Korea (The Republic of Korea). Each country has its own government.

The Korean War broke out between North and South Korea in 1950, when troops from the North invaded the South. Peace talks ended the war but the country still remains divided.

Seoul: the capital city of South Korea.

The history of taekwondo

Some people say that taekwondo can be traced back to about 50 BC. Wall paintings depicting men in fighting **stance** were found in tombs in Korea. However, some people claim the figures are dancing, not fighting.

The Hwa Rang Do were elite nobles devoted to improving their minds and bodies and serving the Kingdom Silla (57 BC – AD 936). Their styles of martial arts included tae kyon and soo bakh do. The philosophy of modern taekwondo is based on these styles.

The techniques of taekwondo are derived from many martial arts, but mainly Okinawan karate. During World War II, Korean soldiers were trained in Japan. They learned karate while they were there and then took their new skills back to Korea. During Japan's occupation of Korea, the Japanese tried to get rid of all Korean culture, which included their martial arts.

After the war, many martial arts (some centuries old) known as 'kwans' sprang up in Korea. To standardize all the different styles, a meeting for kwan masters was held in 1955. They chose the name taekwondo, which describes both foot and hand techniques.

It's a fact!

Taekwondo, tang soo do and hapkido are the three major kicking and punching arts performed in Korea.

In 1973, an international governing body called the World Taekwondo Federation (WTF) was founded. Since then, taekwondo has spread to almost every country in the world and has 20 million followers world-wide. Today, it is the world's most widely practiced martial art.

In 1980, WTF taekwondo was recognized by the International Olympic Committee. In 1988, taekwondo became a demonstration sport at the Olympic games and at the 2000 Olympic Games it will be an Olympic sport.

There are many governing bodies of taekwondo around the world, but the main difference between them is that some, like the WTF, are more interested in full-contact (sparring), while others, like the ITF (International Taekwondo Federation), concentrate on semi-contact.

Kukkiwon is the famous Korean headquarters for taekwondo. Many taekwondo players travel from around the world to train here.

Dress code & etiquette

Dress code

The taekwondo uniform is called a dobok. Like most other martial arts uniforms, a dobok looks like loose-fitting white pajamas with a belt around the waist. The dobok is lightweight and comfortable. There are no zips, buttons or pockets that might cause injury.

A dobok. The pants are tied with a drawstring. The top folds left over right and is tied with a belt. Other tops are simply pulled on over the head.

How to tie your belt.

1 *Hold one end of the belt to one side and take it behind your back.*

2 *Bring the belt around your waist twice.*

3 *Cross the ends over in front of each other.*

4 *Take one end over both lengths of the belt and loop over.*

5 *Cross over the lengths in front of you again.*

6 *Pull tight.*

Etiquette

Taekwondo schools require students to show proper respect for their instructors and training hall (**dojang**). Bowing is the most common way of showing this respect.

Bowing is done:

⊙ when entering and leaving the dojang

⊙ when wanting to speak to an instructor (you must wait for a return bow before you start speaking)

⊙ when receiving awards.

How to bow.

Stand in an attention stance with flat hands against thighs and heels together. Then bow and the instructor bows in return.

Uniforms must always be kept clean and in good repair. When students need to adjust their belt, they must turn and face the back of the hall.

All jewelry, such as rings, necklaces, earrings and bracelets, is removed before entering the dojang. This is to ensure the safety of both yourself and the person you might be training with. Some clubs advise that students leave all jewelry at home for safety reasons. Toenails and fingernails must also be cut short.

Before you start

Choosing a club

There is no worldwide standard for taekwondo. Some clubs have different methods of training and teach their own **forms** or patterns of moves (known as **poomse**). This means that you might join one taekwondo club and be unable to train at another club because they practice different forms. Some clubs will claim that their style is the best. The truth is, only you can decide which club you will be most comfortable with.

A look through the telephone book under the general heading 'Martial Arts' will show you where the nearest clubs are.

It is better to join a large club with many members and other clubs within its organization. Find out if the club has students about your own age. If not, you could always join with a friend.

If money is a consideration, phone around and compare costs. Some clubs charge a joining fee, while other clubs only charge per visit. Visitors normally do not pay, so it is a good idea to sit in on a session or two before joining a club.

As you advance through the grades, you will be required to pass gradings. There are fees attached to these and the costs vary, depending on the grading. As you go up through the grades, the cost also increases.

Joining a taekwondo club can be fun. Club members can sign up for competitions and travel interstate or even overseas. Some clubs take their students away on camps.

15

Clothing

It is not expensive to start taekwondo. Your first few training sessions can be performed in a sweatsuit or loose pants and a T-shirt.

Before paying for a new taekwondo uniform, visit second-hand or recycled clothing stores. Be sure to say that you require a taekwondo uniform. You could even ask the club that you are joining if any older students have uniforms that are now too small for them. This will also save you from having to buy the club's badges and sew them on.

If you buy your uniform new, be sure to order it one size too big. Despite what the manufacturer's label says, they do shrink. You will also need to purchase your new club's badges and the correct belt (usually white) for your uniform.

It is a good idea to buy a mouth-guard from your dentist. These items are especially advised for students who do a lot of **sparring**. Boys who are advanced students may need to wear groin protectors.

'Failure and success
If there is little chance
of success is very

Insurance

Insurance is advised, although you are unlikely to get badly injured at a well-run taekwondo club. Most clubs have insurance cover so it pays to ask.

Confidence and disabilities

Everyone feels nervous when they first enter a dojang under bright lights. Once you have passed your first few belt gradings — everyone passes the early belts — you will feel more confident. If you push yourself to face your fears, it will be easier to overcome them.

A light stretching work-out just before competition is a good way to keep warm and to loosen stiff muscles, which can cause nerves. Good instructors will teach you breathing techniques, which will calm you and help you to focus.

A disability should not stop you from trying taekwondo. Many top athletes have **asthma**. Other athletes have **diabetes**. Getting fit through taekwondo can help improve your overall condition. Just make sure your instructor knows of your complaint, take the necessary precautions and bow out when you do not feel well.

come hand in hand.
of failure, then the joy
small.'

Korean saying

Fitness and training

Beginner martial artists are not usually ready for serious training. This takes time. They need to build fitness slowly. Most martial arts clubs have a beginners' class, where students learn the basic self-defense techniques and get fit.

At the start of each training session, students bow to their instructor. A warm-up follows which involves stretching exercises. The instructor will then teach the class something new or ask the class to practice what they have already learned.

Contests are sometimes part of a training session, and some instructors pick teams to compete against one another.

Stretching

As well as fitness you will need to gain flexibility. This means stretching all your body parts. You need to loosen and warm tight and cold muscles.

It is important to keep each stretching movement gentle and slow. You should not use jerking or bouncing movements.

It is as important to loosen up before training, as it is to cool down when finishing. Taekwondo clubs concentrate on legs, because legwork outweighs handwork. There are a number of ways to stretch your limbs.

1 Hamstring stretch

It is equally important to cool down after exercising. This maintains the level of blood circulation and reduces muscle spasms. Gentle cool-down stretches also help prevent injuries, because they reduce muscle tightness.

Stretching has many purposes. It:
- increases heart and lung capacity
- helps you practice movements you are about to perform
- helps avoid injury from pulled muscles
- gives you greater flexibility.

2 *Hamstring stretch*

4 *Loosening knee joints*

3 *Lateral stretch*

5 *Rolling head to loosen neck*

19

Sparring

Sparring is when students pair off and exchange techniques with each other, usually without the partner knowing the next move. Sparring is practiced in training and it is important as it teaches students which techniques will work in real-life situations (as well as in competitions).

Students should know how to take a hit, as well as how to deliver one. However, most taekwondo clubs do not teach full-contact sparring.

*In sparring, students pair off against a real opponent. Without prearranged moves, they practice what they have learned in their **poomse**.*

Full contact is not allowed in sparring, although injuries can occur if students do not have control of their actions. Well-run clubs have good protective equipment for students to wear when sparring.

Sparring

Taekwondo techniques

There are dozens of kicks, punches and strikes to learn in taekwondo. You will find some easier to master than others. You should practice even the techniques that you do not like. Every technique defends and counter-attacks an imaginary opponent.

Breaking

Breaking techniques are demonstrations of kicking and punching techniques. They are practiced to demonstrate the student's understanding of power. Usually only senior students get to break boards. Some students can break up to ten boards at a time.

1 Front kick

Students learn the power of their foot and fist work by breaking boards. In all of these moves, the hips are used to give extra power to the strike.

Striking

Striking is done with both hands and feet. When striking, pads are used to focus your attention on an object. Pads can be moved around to sharpen the attacker's reflexes.

Pads can be used for training. The student handling the pads controls the action. Here, the kicker delivers a roundhouse kick.

Side kick

Punch

Knife hand strike

Roundhouse kick

23

Punching techniques

Beginners learn simple punching techniques. Always strike with the first two knuckles, because these are the biggest and strongest. Never bend your wrist when you strike. Keep the wrist in a straight line with your forearm.

Poomse (forms)

Forms, called poomse, are set routines where students practice the skills they have learned. Poomse are a set sequence of moves. Students learn the moves by repetition. Different poomse teach new hand and foot techniques.

Poomse are also performed as exams. To reach black belt status, students usually need to know at least ten poomse. They must show their understanding of each move and execute it with focus and strength.

This student is demonstrating some of the beginner's first poomse.

Tuck all your fingers into your palm, and then curl your thumb over them so that it does not protrude from your fist.

1

2

3

Self-defense techniques

Taekwondo relies mainly on kicking and punching, although close contact work, known as self-defense, is usually taught to higher grade students. The aim of self-defense is to **immobilize** your opponent so that they cannot strike you.

The purpose of self-defense is to recognize and avoid dangerous situations. If a confrontation arises, you can unbalance your opponent in a controlled way. **Sweeping** an opponent's leg out from under them is a good and simple start.

This is usually followed up by a strike of some kind, or an armlock or headlock. The aim is to immobilize your opponent in the most efficient way possible.

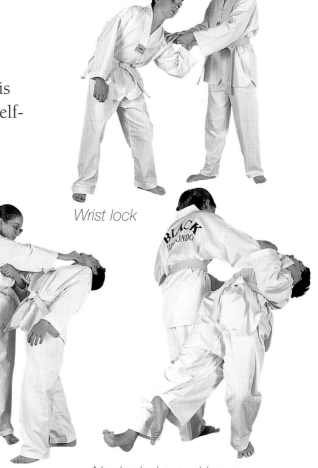

Wrist lock

Neck choke

Neck choke and leg sweep

25

The belt system

The belt system showing the different color levels.

The color of a taekwondo player's belt indicates the standard the wearer has reached. Most martial arts have a belt system but the colors of achievement often vary.

In taekwondo, white belts are worn by beginners and black belts are worn by masters. Grades in-between wear other colors. For each color level there are different grades that students have to pass through. White stripes are added to the colored belts to indicate the grade the student has achieved.

Each colored belt has a meaning. The white belt represents a beginning. The yellow belt stands for the earth and growth. The green belt denotes new growth (not all clubs use a green belt). The blue belt signifies that the wearer is reaching for the sky. The red belt warns of danger, for the wearer knows of many dangerous techniques. Black is the opposite of white, and represents the Yin and the Yang of opposites.

Once you have reached the level of black belt, you move onto dan grades. Dan simply means that you've become a 'serious' student.

To achieve a higher grading, students have to perform poomse. Gradings for higher belts require a student to understand some of the Korean terminology and to perform sparring.

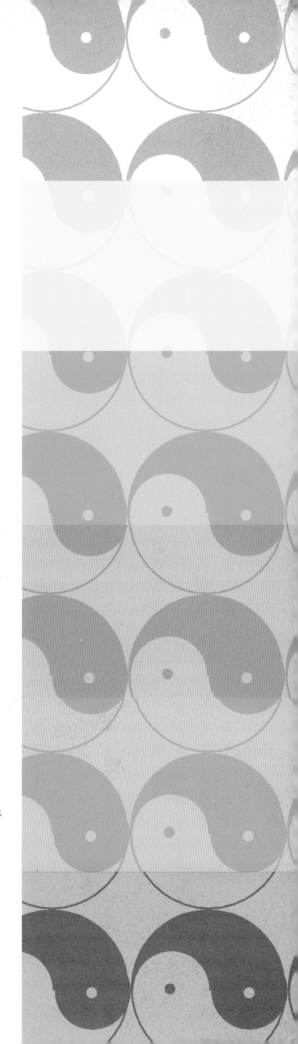

The language of taekwondo

In taekwondo, major commands are spoken in Korean. It is a sign of respect to know Korean, since taekwondo originated in Korea. A taekwondo player can also travel anywhere in the world and understand the basic language of taekwondo.

To learn taekwondo, you will need to learn some of the following expressions. Some of the terms vary from club to club.

dojang	practice gym or training hall
gup/kub	ranks below black belt
dan	black belt and above
poomse	patterns of moves or routines
qwang jung	chief instructor
sa bon nim	instructor
dobok	uniform
charyot	attention
chinna	self-defense
chumbi	'start' command
cha chum sogi	horse-back stance
pyonio sogi	ready stance
shijak	start
gu man	stop
dora	turn
chagi	kick
jurigi	punch
makki	block
dubon	double kick

arra makki	arm or hand block to protect your lower body from attack
olgul makki	arm or hand block across the face
mom ton	arm movement across
makki	body to block attack
ap chagi	front kick
yeop chagi	side kick
dollyo chagi	round kick
shiole	rest
ki	a life energy that is present throughout the universe (*see* kiup)
kiup	a yell made when demonstrating a technique. A student's abdomen contracts and pushes out the ki (energy) from within to add power and focus to a technique. A sudden screamed kiup distracts an opponent and it also reminds students to breathe correctly while practicing martial arts

Counting one to ten

hana	one	1
dul	two	2
set	three	3
net	four	4
dasot	five	5
yasot	six	6
ilgot	seven	7
yardolt	eight	8
a hop	nine	9
yeol	ten	10

Competition taekwondo

Championships are held in big halls. Two judges, who sit in opposite corners, a referee, a timekeeper and a scorer preside over matches.

Competitors display more than just their fighting ability at contests. There are competitions for breaking techniques and poomse.

Taekwondo competition

International competitors have to be 14 years and over to compete in World Taekwondo Federation competitions. In South Korea, there are annual national competitions held at Kukkiwon, the National Taekwondo Center. Some Korean primary schools place great emphasis on taekwondo and have competitive squads.

Many clubs have their own tournaments, while others stage inter-club competitions. Other clubs do not promote competitive taekwondo and choose not to enter tournaments.

Glossary

armlock — applying leverage to an opponent's arm to restrain him or her

asthma — a breathing disorder

diabetes — a disease where the body does not fully take in sugar

dojang — training hall

enlightenment — well-informed

feudal — dating back to the Middle Ages

form — a set pattern of moves to teach you different techniques

immobilize — to hold still or stop movement

indomitable — cannot be overcome

ninja — traditionally a spy or assassin

poomse — pattern or routine of moves

rank — the level of achievement that you have reached, ie, yellow belt, green belt, etc

self-defense — usually grappling, which involves pinning your opponent so that they cannot strike you

sparring — exchanging techniques with a partner, usually without either partner knowing what the other is about to do

stance — a feet and leg position from which punching or kicking is practiced

sweeping — unbalancing your opponent by hooking their foot

Yin and Yang — the two basic principles of the universe in Chinese philosophy. Yin is passive and yielding, whereas Yang is active and assertive

Index